Contemporary CLASSICS

in *Plaids & Stripes*

9 Projects from Piece O′ Cake Designs!

Becky Goldsmith & Linda Jenkins

C&T PUBLISHING

© 2002, Becky Goldsmith & Linda Jenkins
Editor-in-Chief: Darra Williamson
Editor: Amy Marson
Technical Editor: Gailen Runge
Copy editor/Proofreader: Susan Nelsen
Cover Designer: Kristen Yenche
Book Designer: Kirstie L. McCormick & Becky Goldsmith
Illustrator: Becky Goldsmith
Production Assistant: Kirstie L. McCormick
Photography: Sharon Risedorph
Published by C&T Publishing, Inc., P.O. Box 1456, Lafayette, California 94549
Front cover images: *Pretty in Plaid* by Becky Goldsmith pg 43
Back cover images: *Tossed Tulips* by Linda Jenkins and *Waltzing Stars* by Becky Goldsmith

Library of Congress Cataloging-in-Publication Data

Goldsmith, Becky
  Contemporary classics in plaids & stripes : 9 projects from Piece 'O
Cake Designs / Becky Goldsmith & Linda Jenkins.
      p. cm.
Includes index.
  ISBN 1-57120-205-6 (paper trade)
  1. Patchwork--Patterns. 2. Appliqué--Patterns. 3. Quilts. 4.
Plaid. 5. Stripes. I. Title: Contemporary classics in plaids and
stripes. II. Jenkins, Linda III. Piece 'O Cake Designs. IV. Title.

  TT835 .G654497 2003
  746.46'041--dc21

                                    2002151617

Printed in USA
10 9 8 7 6 5 4 3 2 1

DEDICATION

The first woven plaids we bought were designed by Roberta Horton. Thank you, Roberta, for bringing plaids and stripes back to life in the quilt world!

We wouldn't be where we are without the support of our loving husbands, Steve Goldsmith and Paul Jenkins. Truth be told, we're each pretty pampered. Steve does all the cooking for Becky, and Paul does the bulk of the cleaning and laundry for Linda. And that's in addition to being great guys. We know we are lucky!

We have had some wonderful women working in our office over the years. We are grateful to each of them for their hard work and enthusiasm. We especially thank Dorothy and Gail, our Tulsa staff.

ACKNOWLEDGMENTS

Many thanks to P&B Textiles for working with us to produce a great new collection of woven plaids and stripes! P&B found a weaver who could weave plaids that were neither too heavy nor too light. They are perfect! We hope that you love them as much as we do. We used these plaids and stripes in each of the quilts in this book.

We would also like to thank Hobbs Processing Company for providing us with the 100% organic cotton batting that we used in these quilts.

A NOTE TO OUR READERS...

How many of you pay attention to who publishes the quilt books that you buy and love and use? Over the last several years we, as Piece O' Cake Designs, have self-published all but two of our books and all of our patterns. There has been a Piece O' Cake office that you could call. Many of you have gotten to know our office staff.

Self-publishing and maintaining an office take an enormous amount of time and energy. We finally realized that there is just not time enough in the day to get it all done and still have time to make new and interesting quilts. (Not to mention the fact that our husbands were starting to forget what we looked like.)

We are very happy to announce that we have joined the C&T Publishing family. Their books are both beautiful and well done. We look forward to working with them. It's an added bonus that everyone we've worked with at C&T is just so nice! C&T will distribute all of the Piece O' Cake designs, both old and new, that you love.

We are truly happy about this change in our lives. We are using the time saved to make new quilts! We are still traveling and teaching. You can still contact us if you have questions. It is our hope that, beginning with this book, Piece O' Cake gets even better!

OUR FAVORITE SUPPLIES

Clear, heavy weight self-laminating sheets – Used to make templates. You can find them at most office supply stores and sometimes at warehouse markets. If laminate is hard to find, you can use clear Contac® paper as a substitute.

Clear upholstery vinyl – 54" wide medium weight clear vinyl used to make a positioning overlay. You can usually find it in stores that carry upholstery fabric or in hardware stores. This is the stuff that your grandmother covered her sofa with in the 1950's.

Cotton quilting gloves – These gloves make it easier to hold onto the quilt during machine quilting.

Fabric – All of the fabrics used in this book are 100% cotton.

Fusible web – For those times when you are really in a hurry. There are several brands on the market. Choose the one you like the best and follow the directions on the package.

Needles for hand applique – Linda uses a size 12 John James sharp, and Becky uses a size 11 Hemmings straw needle. There are lots of good needles. Find the one that fits your hand.

Ott light – These lamps give off a bright and natural light. The floor lamp is particularly nice as you can position it over your left shoulder (if you are right-handed). Applique is so much easier when you can see what you are doing!

Pencils – We use either a General's charcoal white chalk pencil or a Quilter's Ultimate mechanical pencil when drawing around templates onto the fabric.

Permanent marker – An ultra fine point Sharpie® marker writes best on the upholstery vinyl.

Rotary cutting mat, ruler, & rotary cutter – A big mat, a variety of rulers, and a sharp rotary cutter will make your life easier.

Sandpaper board – For tracing templates onto fabric. You will love the way the sandpaper holds the fabric in place as you trace around the templates.
Tip: If your sandpaper board is too rough, sand it down with a piece of sandpaper.

Scissors – Embroidery-size scissors for both paper and fabric. Small scissors are better for intricate cutting.

Sequin pins - $1/2"$ – To pin your applique in place.

Sewing machine – You need a sewing machine that is in good working order for piecing. A modern machine is better for machine quilting.

Thread – Use 100% cotton thread with cotton fabric.

Wooden toothpick – Used to help turn the seam allowance under at points and on curves. The wood has a texture that grabs and holds the seam allowance. They work best if you wet them a little in your mouth before each use. We like the round wooden toothpicks with the carved ends that you can find at a Cracker Barrel restaurant or at an Asian grocery store.

TABLE OF CONTENTS

CONTEMPORARY CLASSICS

We love old quilts and often use them as a starting point when designing new quilts. We want the quilts in this book to feel as if they have one foot in the past and one in the now.

One sure way to give a quilt a contemporary attitude is with color. Clear, happy colors feel more like today than "yesterday." The combination of prints, plaids, stripes, and solids in these fresh colors is stimulating - even in what is at heart a traditional design.

What's so special about plaids?

Visual Color Blending

If you are reading this, you love fabric. You probably have lots of fabric, and you still want more! You aren't alone. If you are a quilter, this is just the way you are. That said, do you ever stop and think about why you choose the fabrics you do?

Most of us buy prints. Fabric companies make more prints than anything else. Simply stated, printed fabric has a design "printed" on a base cloth that is already woven. The design can be little bunnies or bunches of flowers or rocks or water - it can be anything. A printed design can be made up of two colors or twenty colors - but these colors are always printed on top of the base cloth.

Woven plaids and stripes are special because the threads in the cloth itself are dyed different colors and then woven together. The magic happens when the colors mix in the fabric.

When two colors are woven together, they make a third color. For example, when blue is woven with red it makes purple. But that purple is not like a printed shade of purple. If you look closely at the fabric, you can still see the blue and the red threads. Your eyes blend the colors for you so that you see purple.

Let's take this blue and red color combination a little bit farther. The blue and the red can come in all sorts of shades. The blue can be dark or light, a true blue or teal. The red can be fire engine red or more of a wine color. The specific shade and value of the colors blend to create subtle and sometimes surprising new colors.

We find that woven plaids and stripes are the best "blenders" in our fabric stash. Let's say you are making a blue and red quilt. You have chosen prints that are predominantly blue and others that are predominantly red. Adding a woven plaid that has both blue and red in it will help you to blend the two colors together.

Woven fabrics can be simple or complex - made up of two colors or twenty colors. The pattern can be large or small. We buy them all.

What about those lines?

By their nature, woven plaids and stripes are directional - there is an easily discernable line in the fabric. This makes some quilters nervous. They think that if the lines in the plaids are not exactly straight, their quilt won't be "right." Well, we are here to tell you that just isn't true!

All fabric has a grain line. When you cut fabric for piecing, you usually want it to be on the straight of grain. When you cut printed fabric you do your best to stay on-grain, but you don't loose sleep over being gently off-grain. The same is true of plaids and stripes. Look closely at our quilts and you'll see that the lines in the plaids and stripes are not absolutely on the straight of grain. We feel like that makes the quilt more interesting to look at.

Applique pieces are usually cut on the bias. The only time this is not true is if there is a design in the fabric that you want to take advantage of and fussy cut it. We treat prints and plaids the same way.

The two stars at left are from the quilt Neapolitan Nights. Notice that by "fussy cutting" the plaid and striped fabric, you can create exciting patterns inside the stars.

Opposites Attract

We all know it's true. We mix salty with sweet, hot with cold, tall with short, the list goes on and on. The contrasts make things more interesting. In quilts we mix light with dark. It is this contrast that creates the pattern in the quilt.

We also mix curves with straight lines in the quilt top. Most quilters are used to doing this with their quilting stitches. The conventional wisdom holds that if you have a pieced quilt, the quilting should be curvy. Applique quilts with their sinuous designs often have straight lines in their quilting.

We like the combination of curvy prints with plaids and stripes. The interplay between the straight and curved lines add visual interest to the quilt. Combine that with the magic colors in the plaids and stripes and you just can't go wrong.

FOR YOUR INFORMATION...

Fabric Preparation

Use 100% cotton fabric. Cotton has withstood the test of time, and it is easy to work with. It is easy to find and reasonably priced.

We pre-wash all of our fabric. If it is going to shrink or bleed we want to know that before it ruins a quilt. Pre-washed fabric has a better hand and is easier to applique than unwashed fabric. And, last but not least, fabric that has been washed smells a lot better.

About Our Fabric Requirements

Cotton fabric is 40"-44" wide off the bolt. To be safe, we calculated our fabric requirements based on a 40" width.

Many of the quilts in this book can be called "scrap quilts". They are made from small amounts of many different fabrics. Fabric is sold off the bolt in increments of $1/8$ yard, $1/4$ yard, etc. If you need to cut a piece for a scrap quilt 5" x 8" you would need to buy at least $1/4$ yard. You will have fabric left over.

What we have done in our fabric requirements is tell you how much yardage you would need if you were cutting that piece from only one fabric. Use the fabric requirements for each quilt as a guide, but remember that the yardage amounts you need for your quilt will vary depending on the number of fabrics you use and the size of the pieces you cut from them. We have included in the measurements a little room for shrinkage.

About the Big Pattern Page

There is a large pattern sheet in this book. To remove it, carefully tear it along the perforations. Most of the applique patterns are printed on this sheet. Each pattern is labeled, numbered, and the horizontal and vertical centers are marked.

You will make copies of the patterns to make your templates. Fold the large pattern page wherever you have to so that it will fit on a copier. Re-fold as necessary.

Seam Allowances

Be accurate in your piecing! These patterns are designed with a $1/4$" seam allowance in mind. If your seam allowance varies from this, your quilt top may not fit together.

The cutting instructions in this book are mathematically correct. For example, the border lengths for Waltzing Stars are calculated for 12" blocks. However, those blocks are heavily pieced and can draw up - even when stitched on foundation papers. Remember to always measure your quilt and cut sashing and borders to fit it. The measurements provided should be very close to your actual quilt size.

GENERAL APPLIQUE INSTRUCTIONS

Preparing Backgrounds for Applique

Always cut your background fabric larger than the size it will be when it is pieced into the quilt. The outer edges of your block can stretch and fray when you handle it while stitching. Your applique can shift during stitching and can cause your block to shrink slightly. For these reasons it is best to add 1" to all sides of your backgrounds when you cut them out. The cutting instructions include this additional fabric.

Press each background block in half vertically and horizontally. This establishes a center grid in your background. This pressed grid will line up with the center grid on your positioning overlay. When your background is pieced, as it is in *Simplicity* and *Pretty in Plaid*, the seam lines are your grid lines.

Make Your Positioning Overlay

The positioning overlay is used to place each applique piece accurately on the block. It is easy to make and use. The overlay makes your projects very portable.

Cut a piece of clear upholstery vinyl, with its tissue paper lining, to the finished size of each block. Set the tissue paper aside until you are ready to fold or store your overlay. Make copies of the patterns in this book to work from. Where necessary, tape the pattern pages together.

Tape the copy of a pattern onto the table in front of you. Tape the upholstery vinyl over it. Using a ruler and an ultra fine point Sharpie® marker, draw a line on the vinyl over the horizontal and vertical center lines on your pattern.

Trace the pattern accurately onto the vinyl. The numbers on the pattern indicate stitching sequence. Include these numbers on your overlay.

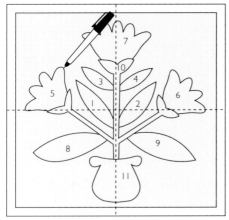

Tape the upholstery vinyl over the pattern.

Trace the pattern onto the vinyl.

Make Your Templates

Each applique shape requires a template. We have a different way to make templates that is both easy and accurate. Make two to five copies of each applique block on a copier. Compare your copies with the original to ensure that they are accurate.

From these copies cut out each shape for which you need a template. Leave a little paper allowance around these shapes. Where one shape lays over another, cut the top shape from one copy and the bottom shape from another copy.

Take one clear heavyweight self-laminating sheet (available at most office supply stores) and lay it shiny side down on the table in front of you. Peel the paper backing off leaving the sticky side up. Carefully stick each paper template with the drawn side down to the laminate. Use more laminating sheets as necessary.

Cut out each template. Try to split the drawn line – don't cut inside or outside of the line. Keep edges smooth and points sharp.

You'll notice how easy these templates are to cut out. Your hands won't hurt from cutting lots of templates. That's the main reason we like this method. It is also true that a mechanical copy of the pattern is more accurate than hand tracing onto template plastic. As you use the templates you will see that they are sturdy and hold up to repeated use.

Using Templates

In hand applique, templates are used right side up, on the right side of the fabric. Begin by laying your applique fabric right side up on a sandpaper board. Lay your template right side up on the fabric. Lay the template so that as many edges as possible are on the diagonal grain of the fabric. (A bias edge is easier to turn under than one that is on the straight of grain.)

Trace around the template with a mechanical or chalk pencil. Keep this drawn line as close to the template as you can. Cut each fabric applique piece out, adding a $^3/_{16}$" seam allowance.

Using the Positioning Overlay

Finger-press the seam allowance of the applique pieces under before positioning them on your block. This is a very important step. As you finger-press, make sure that the drawn line is finger-pressed to the back. You'll be amazed at how much easier this one step makes turning under the seam allowance. For more information on finger-pressing, see page 13.

To use the overlay, lay your background right side up on your sandpaper board. Place the overlay over it, also right side up. Line up the center grids. You will slide each applique piece, right side up, under the overlay but on top of the background fabric, one piece at a time. It is easy to tell when the applique pieces are in position under the overlay.

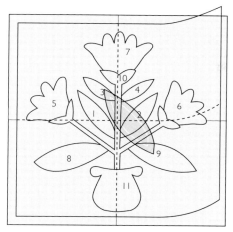

Line up the center grids on the vinyl and the background fabric. Slide piece #1 under the vinyl.

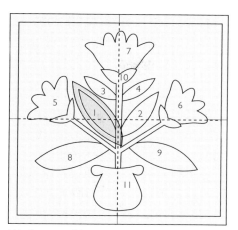

Work piece #1 into position. Pin it in place and remove the vinyl.

Pin your applique pieces in place using ¹/₂" sequin pins. We generally position and stitch only one or two pieces at a time. Remove the vinyl overlay before stitching.

When you are ready to put away the overlay, lay the tissue paper over the drawn side before you fold it. The tissue paper keeps the lines from transferring from one part of the vinyl to another.

Applique Your Blocks

Hand applique your pieces in place with an invisible stitch and matching thread. Refer to *The Applique Sampler* by Piece O' Cake for more details on needleturn applique.

> **FYI...**
> **We don't trim away fabric from behind our applique. We believe that leaving the background intact makes the quilt stronger. And, should the quilt ever need repair, it's better if the background has not been cut.**

Trimming the Applique Blocks

After your applique is complete, gently press your blocks on the wrong side. If your ironing surface is hard, lay your blocks on a towel and your applique will not get flattened. Trim your blocks to the size indicated in the pattern. Always make sure that your design is properly centered and aligned with your ruler before you cut off the excess fabric. Assemble your quilt top as directed.

Fusible Applique Instructions

Templates for Fusible Applique

Make your templates as stated on page 10, with one exception. Stick the **blank** side of the paper copies to the sticky side of the laminate. You will use the templates shiny side up.

Using Templates in Fusible Applique

Templates are used on the wrong side of the fabric in fusible applique. Following the instructions on your fusible web, iron it to the wrong side of your applique fabric. Do not peel off the paper backing.

Lay the prepared fabric right side down. Lay your template in place with the drawn side down, the shiny side up. Trace around the template onto the paper backing. Cut out your applique pieces on the drawn line. Peel off the paper backing when you are ready to fuse.

Positioning Overlay with Fusible Applique

Make the overlay as directed on page 9. Prepare the applique pieces for fusing. Lay your background fabric right side up on your ironing board. Place the overlay over it, also right side up. Line up the center grids. Slide each applique piece, right side up, under the overlay but on top of the background fabric, one piece at a time. This step is illustrated on page 11. In fusible applique you can position many pieces at once.

Carefully remove the overlay. Do not touch the overlay vinyl with the iron because it will melt. Following the directions on the fusible web, iron the applique pieces in place.

Finish the Edges

After fusing cotton fabric, we finish the raw edges of the fused applique on the sewing machine. As the quilts are used, the stitching keeps the edges secure. The stitching you use can be subtle or very decorative - from a straight stitch in matching thread to an embroidery stitch in contrasting thread. Choose stitching that works with your quilt best.

Trim your blocks to size as directed previously.

Applique Tips & Techniques

Finger-Pressing

We do needleturn hand applique. Trust us, we have heard every possible variation for hand applique, and this is still our favorite technique. The templates are easy to make and they are reusable. The overlay makes positioning applique pieces accurate, and it's easy to take your project along wherever you go. There is not a lot of *stuff* to do to get ready to stitch.

There is one trick, though, that makes needleturning very easy. That trick is finger-pressing. We mentioned finger-pressing on page 10, but it's important enough to mention again. If you skip this step, it actually makes the stitching *slower* because you have to work harder to turn your edges under neatly.

Finger-press **every applique piece** before positioning it on your block. Good-quality 100% cotton fabric has a memory and holds a crease very well. To finger-press, hold the applique piece right side up. Using your thumb and index finger turn the seam allowance to the back so that the chalk line is just barely turned under. Use your fingers to "press" a crease into the fabric along the inside of the chalk line. Finger-press every edge that will be sewn down.

Clipping Inner Points

You have to clip an inner point before you can turn it. When you can no longer turn the seam allowance under smoothly, it is time to clip the inner point. Always make your clip straight into the point - do not clip at an angle. Cut to and just barely through the chalk line.

Take a moment to consider how scissors work. The cut is made where the two scissor blades meet. When you clip, you can only see the top blade. **The cut is made on the left side of that top blade.**

When you clip, carefully position the cutting edge of the top scissor blade where you want the cut to be.

Cutaway Applique

Cutaway applique is a technique that makes small, narrow, pointy, or oddly-shaped pieces easier to handle. Leaving surplus fabric around the applique shape gives you more to hold on to, gives you room to pin, and reduces fraying. Remember to finger-press before positioning your piece on the block!

Lay the stem template right side up on the diagonal grain of the stem fabric (also right side up). Trace around the template.

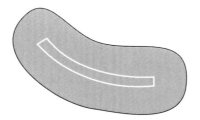

Cut the stem out leaving about 1" of fabric all the way around it. Finger-press the stem on the chalk line.

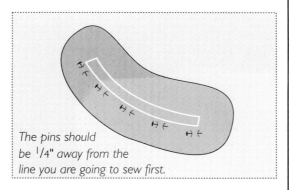

The pins should be 1/4" away from the line you are going to sew first.

Use the overlay to position the stem on your block. Sew the concave side of a stem first if you can. Notice that the pins are not going down the center of the stem — there would be no room to turn under the seam allowance!

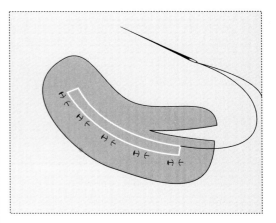

Cut away 2"-3" on the concave side of the stem, leaving a 3/16" seam allowance. Begin sewing at the base of the stem. If the ends of the stem are covered by another applique piece, they do not need to be turned under.

Continue cutting away a little and sewing a little until you reach the end of the concave side of the stem. Knot your thread and then begin again on the other side of the stem.

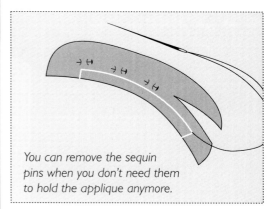

You can remove the sequin pins when you don't need them to hold the applique anymore.

Don't travel with your thread from one side of the stem to the other. It is too easy to distort your applique.

Outer Curves and Circles

The trick to outer curves and circles is to take one stitch at a time. You can only control one stitch at a time. Smooth out the pleats that form using your needle or a wooden toothpick (it really works!). Practice makes perfect. Remember to finger-press.

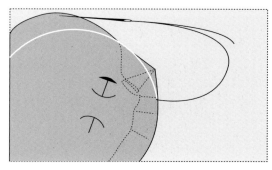

Pleats will form in the seam allowance. This is what causes those points to form at the outer edge of a curve.

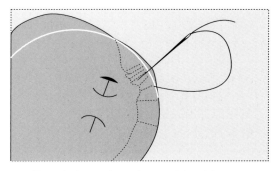

Reach into the pleat with either your needle or your toothpick and smooth it out. Work the fabric in the pleat back and forth a bit.

As you work with the pleat, the outer edge will smooth out.

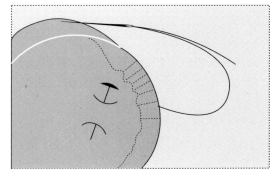

Once the pleat is smoothed out, continue sewing. When another pleat forms, repeat the process.

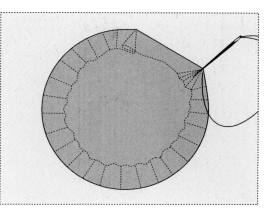

When you are within a few stitches from the end of a circle, you must turn under the remaining seam allowance.

This forms two pleats with a flat space between them - three things to fix! Use your needle or a wooden toothpick to fan open the first pleat.

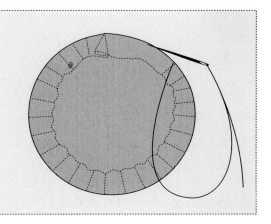

Once the first pleat has been dealt with you can sometimes take a stitch or two. Then you must deal with the flat space.

Use the tip of the needle to grab the top edge of the circle and lift it up. The edge of the circle should round itself out along the finger-pressed fold.

Fan open the last pleat and complete the circle.

Making Continuous Bias for Stems & Binding

We find this method for making continuous bias to be particularly easy. A surprisingly small amount of fabric makes quite a bit of bias.

Begin with a square of fabric. Choose the size of the square from the chart below to make 1 1/2" wide bias for bias stems.

12" square makes 80"
18" square makes 200"
24" square makes 360"
30" square makes 580"

Make 2 1/2" wide continuous bias for binding:

19" square makes 125"
24" square makes 180"
30" square makes 320"
36" square makes 500"

Cut the square in half diagonally.

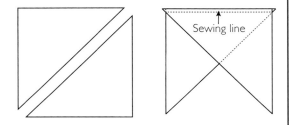

Sewing line

Sew the two triangles together, right sides together, as shown. Remember that when you make continuous bias you are always sewing together fabric that is on the straight of grain.

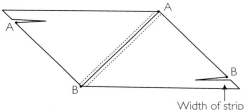

A   A   B   B
Width of strip

Press the seam allowance open.

Make a 4" long cut into two sides of the fabric as shown. Make the cut the width you want your bias strip to be (1 1/2" or 2 1/2").

Match the points marked A and the points marked B together, with the fabric right sides together.

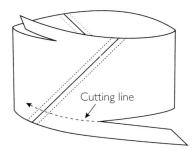

A's
B's

Sew the two edges together to form a tube. Press the seam open.

Cutting line

Using your rotary cutter and ruler, cut a continuous bias strip off of the edge of the tube you have constructed.

Press the strip wrong sides together, lengthwise for binding and for bias stem.

FYI...

Try putting a small rotary mat on the round end of your ironing board. Then slide the tube of fabric over it. Use a ruler and rotary cutter to cut the long strip of continuous bias. Rotate the tube of fabric as necessary.

If your ironing board is padded, the very hard. Cut using a gentle pressure with the rotary cutter.

Bias Stem

This is a great technique when you need long stems of a uniform width. We used bias stems in the borders of *Pretty in Plaid*, *Simplicity*, and *Waltzing Stars*.

Use your overlay to position these longs stems on you border background. We find it easier to first pin the stem in place and then baste it.

Lightly press your continuous bias strip lengthwise, wrong sides together.

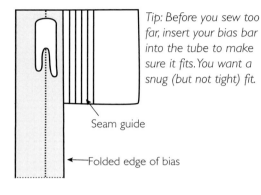

Tip: Before you sew too far, insert your bias bar into the tube to make sure it fits. You want a snug (but not tight) fit.

Seam guide

Folded edge of bias

Place the folded edge of the bias strip against the seam guide of your sewing machine. Find the width of the stem you want to make. For example, if you are making 1/4" bias stem, place the folded edge at the 1/4" mark.

Sew down the length of the strip.

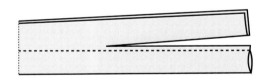

Trim away excess fabric, leaving a very scant seam allowance.

Insert the rounded end of the 1/4" bias bar into your sewn bias tube. Shift the seam and seam allowance to the back of the bar and press it in place.

Work the bar down the length of the bias tube, pressing as you go. Remove the bias bar.

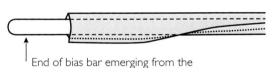

End of bias bar emerging from the far end of the bias tube

Hold up the finished bias stem. You'll notice that it wants to curve in one direction more than the other.

The side closest to the seam line makes the tighter curve. When possible, match this side of the bias stem to the concave side of the stem on your pattern.

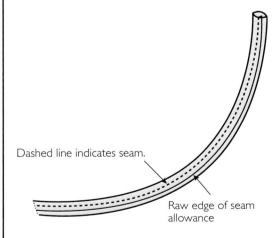

Dashed line indicates seam.

Raw edge of seam allowance

PIECING TIPS & TECHNIQUES

Triangle Squares

Many of the quilts in this book have triangle squares. These triangle squares have a light side and a dark side. The cutting directions for each quilt will tell you how many squares and what size to cut. Make your triangle squares as directed below.

Cut the required number of light and dark squares in the size directed.

Lay a light square over a dark square, right sides together. Sew on the diagonal. Repeat for all squares.

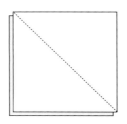

Cut the excess fabric ¼" away from your seam line, as shown below.

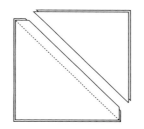

Press seams to the dark side unless otherwise indicated.

Here's a neat trick for sewing the diagonal line without marking! Put a piece of paper (or a ruler) squarely on the bed of your sewing machine. Line up one side of the paper with the spot where the needle makes its stitch.

Stick a 3"-4" length of blue painter's tape on the table (not the throat plate) in line with the edge of the paper. The edge of the tape will be aligned with the stitching path.

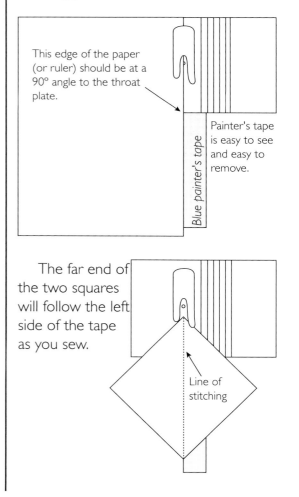

This edge of the paper (or ruler) should be at a 90° angle to the throat plate.

Blue painter's tape

Painter's tape is easy to see and easy to remove.

The far end of the two squares will follow the left side of the tape as you sew.

Line of stitching

Triangle Corners

Triangle corners are made in much the same way triangle squares are made. We added triangle corners to the Snowball blocks in *Meadow Green* and to the blocks in the borders of *The Delectable Mountains*.

Cut the required number of small and large squares in the sizes directed.

Lay a small square over a large square, right sides together. Sew on the diagonal. Repeat for all large squares.

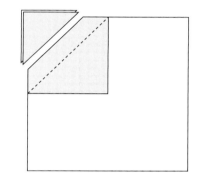

Use the painter's tape trick shown on the previous page when sewing the diagonal seam.

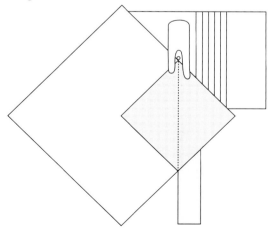

Cut the excess fabric ¹/4" away from your seam line, as shown below.

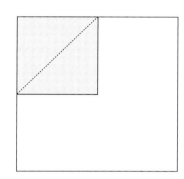

Press seams to the dark side unless otherwise indicated.

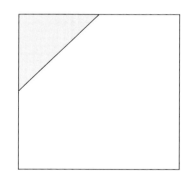

Repeat for the opposite corner. If the pattern calls for four triangle corners repeat for the other two corners of the block.

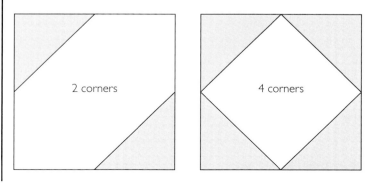

2 corners

4 corners

Pieced Nine-Patches

The Nine-Patch is such a versatile block! It can be combined with other blocks to create many different attitudes. We used Nine-Patches in *Tossed Tulips, Royal Plumes,* and *Meadow Green.* Each of these quilts has a scrappy mix of fabrics.

We wanted to achieve a scrappy look in these quilts and still maintain the ease of strip piecing. To do this we cut shorter strips (20" long instead of 40") in several different fabrics. Here's how we did it:

Cut the designated number of light and dark strips in the size directed in the pattern. Make the designated number of dark-light-dark strips. Press seam allowances to the dark side.

Cut off the designated number of units. These units will be the same width as the light or dark strips. For example, if your strips were cut 2" wide, the units you cut off will be 2" wide.

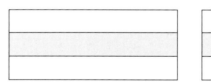

Make the designated number of light-dark-light strips. Press seam allowances to the dark side.

Cut off the designated number of units. These units will be the same width as the light or dark strips.

Combine units to make the Nine-Patch blocks. Some Nine-Patches will have more dark squares. Other Nine-Patches will have more light squares. Make the light and dark Nine-Patches called for in the pattern.

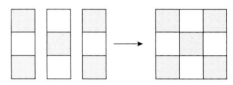

Nine-Patch with more dark squares

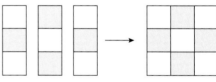

Nine-Patch with more light squares

FYI...

There are two ways to match up the points in a Nine-Patch. When the fabrics in the strip are pressed to the darker fabric, a ridge is created. When you place your units right sides together, those ridges bump up next to each other. Often you can bump them together, pin them in place, and sew.

However, if your points are not matching up well, use a positioning pin (next page) to make sure that these seams are where they are supposed to be.

Positioning Pins

You know how tricky it can be to match points in piecing. Use a positioning pin to match your points before you sew them together. This technique is especially useful when matching the points of triangle squares or when sewing together the blocks in *Waltzing Stars*.

We'll use two Lady of the Lake blocks as an example. Use positioning pins to match the points where the blocks are sewn together.

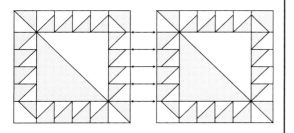

The blocks are sewn right sides together. You'll be looking at the wrong side of the block on top which means that the seam allowances will keep you from seeing the pointy-est part of the point.

Insert the pin into the point from the back side of the top block. Then look at it from the front to make sure you are actually in the point. Next, insert the pin into the matching point in the second block.

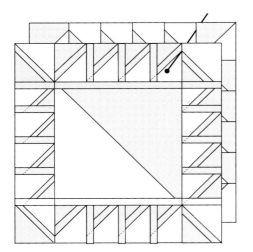

Slide the two points together on the positioning pin. Pin the blocks together on either side of the positioning pin. Be careful not to shift the points out of place. Remove the positioning pin.

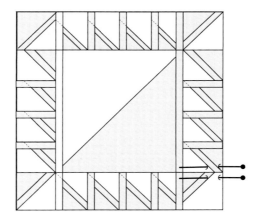

Pin all points in this manner. Sew the blocks together. While we don't usually recommend sewing over pins, it helps to do so here. If you remove the pins too soon, the points shift out of position. We find that we can sew over a pin if we sew slowly and carefully.

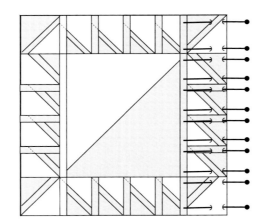

TOSSED TULIPS

Finished applique block size: 6"
Finished pieced border width: 2"
Finished pink middle border width: 1"
Finished outer border width: 2"
Finished quilt size: 58" square

Fresh tulips dance happily in a field of green (see page 34). The prints and plaids are delightfully scrappy. The easy strip-pieced setting combined with the cute appliqued tulips make this quilt a winner!

Materials

Light stripe block backgrounds: 1 $^3/_4$ yards
Light plaid used in the piecing: 1 yard
Green fabrics used in the piecing: 1 yard
Pink middle border fabric: $^1/_2$ yard
Green outer border fabric: $^2/_3$ yard
Applique: A variety of fabric scraps in varying sizes
Binding: $^7/_8$ yard
Backing and sleeve: 4 yards
Batting: 64" square

Cutting Instructions

Block backgrounds
  Cut 35 squares 8" × 8"
Light plaid used in the Nine-Patches and pieced inner border
  Cut 24 strips 2 $^1/_2$" × 20"
Green fabrics used in the Nine-Patches and pieced inner border
  Cut 24 strips 2 $^1/_2$" × 20"
Pink middle border fabric
  Cut 8 strips 1 $^1/_2$" × 40"
    Sew the strips together in pairs. Cut as indicated on page 24.
Green outer border fabric
  Cut 8 strips 2 $^1/_2$" × 40"
    Sew the strips together in pairs. Cut as indicated on page 24.
Binding
  Cut a 30" square to make 2 $^1/_2$" wide continuous bias binding
    (See page 16 for instructions.)

Tossed Tulips Applique Pattern

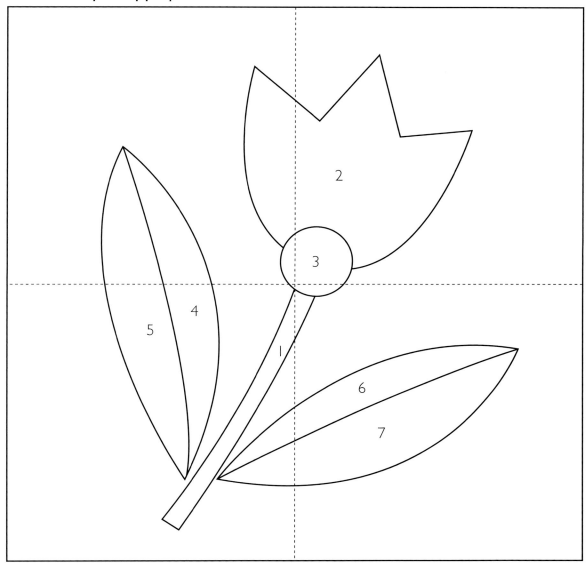

Make the Quilt

Prepare your templates and overlay. "Audition" your applique pieces on the backgrounds on the design wall before you begin stitching. It's a lot easier to change fabrics before they are sewn down.

Applique your blocks. When your applique is complete, press your blocks on the wrong side. Trim the applique blocks to 6 1/2" square.

Strip piece the Nine-Patches (see pages 20 and 24). The more you mix up the combination of green fabric strips, the scrappier your quilt will be. Sew the Nine-Patches as shown on the next page. Use the same units that you constructed the Nine-Patches from to make the inner borders.

Set the quilt together as shown on page 24. Pay very close attention to the placement of the darks and lights inside the pieced Nine-Patches and inner borders. Finish your quilt as directed on pages 54-55.

Make 8 dark-light-dark @ 2 ¹/₂" x 20"
Cut into 60 units 2 ¹/₂" wide.

Make 8 light-dark-light @ 2 ¹/₂" x 20"
Cut into 61 units 2 ¹/₂" wide.

Refer to page 20 for more information on construcing Nine-Patches.

Make 15 dark Nine-Patches.

Make 14 light Nine-Patches.

Make 2 side inner borders sewing 2 ¹/₂" wide units end-to-end as shown above.

Make the top and bottom inner borders sewing 2 ¹/₂" wide units end-to-end as shown above. Remove 1 light square from the far right unit.

FYI...

This quilt has a lot of piecing. If your seam allowance is not exactly ¹/₄", it can greatly affect the overall dimensions of the quilt, so measure the height and width of your quilt before cutting the outer borders to size.

Set the center of the quilt together as shown at right. Attach the pieced inner borders.

Sew the pink middle border strips together end-to-end in pairs. Repeat for the outer border strips. Sew border strips together as shown at right.

Trim the outer borders as directed at right. Attach the outer borders in the following sequence:
1. top
2. right side
3. bottom
4. left side.

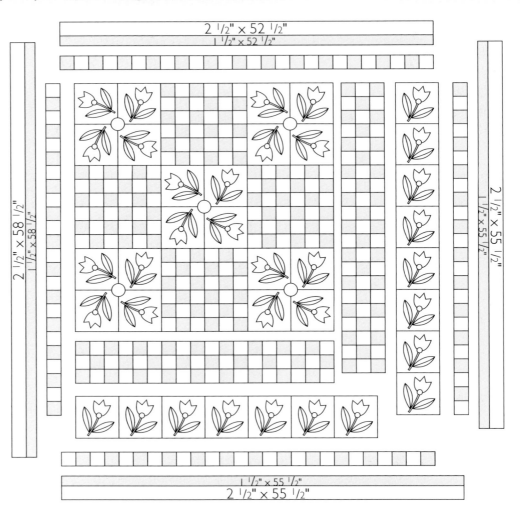

ROYAL PLUMES

Finished applique block size: 9"
Finished Nine-Patches: 3"
Finished inner border width: 1"
Finished outer border width: 2"
Finished quilt size: 36" square

We combined Nine-Patches and applique in this perky little quilt (refer to color image on page 38). This is a "planned" scrappy quilt. The colors in the Nine-Patches and in the borders are mostly random. However, the positioning of the dark rose triangle squares in the centers and corners of the borders combined with the blues in the plumes and the inner border create a subtle square-in-a-square design.

Materials

Light stripe used in piecing and block backgrounds: 1 1/2 yards
Colorful plaids and stripes used in Nine-Patches and triangle squares: 3/4 yard
Blue inner border: 1/4 yard
Applique: A variety of fabric scraps in varying sizes
Plaid binding: 3/4 yard
Backing and sleeve: 1 1/2 yards
Batting: 42" square

Cutting Instructions

Light stripe
Cut 16 squares 6" x 6" for pieced background of applique blocks
Cut 6 strips 1 1/2" x width of fabric for Nine-Patches
    Subcut strips in half (at least 20"), discard 1
Cut 32 setting squares 3 1/2" x 3 1/2"
Cut 68 squares 2 1/2" x 2 1/2" for triangle squares

Colorful plaids and stripes
Cut 7 strips 1 1/2" width of fabric for Nine-Patches
    Subcut strips in half (at least 20"), discard 1
Cut 68 squares 2 1/2" x 2 1/2" for triangle squares

Blue inner border
Cut 2 strips 1 1/2" x 30 1/2" for the side inner borders
Cut 2 strips 1 1/2" x 32 1/2" for the top and bottom inner borders

Plaid binding
Cut a 24" square to make 2 1/2"-wide continuous bias binding
    (See page 16 for instructions.)

Make the Quilt

The pattern for the applique blocks can be found on the large pattern sheet at the back of the book. Prepare your templates and overlay. "Audition" your applique pieces on the backgrounds on the design wall before you begin stitching. We alternated the direction of the stripe in the background. It's a lot easier to change fabrics before they are sewn down. When you are happy with the arrangement of the backgrounds, sew them together into four Four-Patch blocks.

Applique your blocks. When your applique is complete, press your blocks on the wrong side. Trim the applique blocks to 9 ½" square.

Strip piece the Nine-Patches (see page 20 and below). The more you mix up the combination of colorful plaid and striped fabric strips, the scrappier your quilt will be. Make the triangle squares (see page 18).

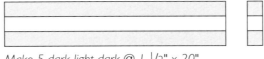

Make 5 dark-light-dark @ 1 ½" x 20"
Cut into 64 units 1 ½" wide.

Make 3 light-dark-light @ 1 ½" x 20"
Cut into 32 units 1 ½" wide.

Make 32 dark Nine-Patches.

Make 68 triangle squares from the dark and the light 2 ½" squares.

FYI...
This quilt has a lot of piecing. If your seam allowance is not exactly ¼", it can greatly affect the overall dimensions of the quilt. Be accurate! Use positioning pins on the points when attaching the borders to the quilt. They will help you sew perfect points.

Position the applique blocks, Nine-Patches, setting blocks, inner border strips, and triangle squares on your design wall. Play with them! You'll be surprised to see how much fun this can be.

When you are happy with the placement of all the elements, set the quilt together as shown below. Finish the quilt as directed on pages 54-55.

WALTZING STARS

Finished star block size: 12"
Finished inner border width: 3/4"
Finished border width: 4"
Finished quilt size: 57 1/2" square

Wowie Zowie! Yellow does perk up a quilt! These stars are a contemporary version of an old favorite, Tennessee Waltz (see page 33). When pieced on foundation papers, the narrow points are easy to piece. Becky used three different yellow prints and many different rose/reds in the pieced stars. The gentle curves in the border help to soften the pointy-ness of the stars.

Materials
Yellow block and border backgrounds: 5 1/2 yards
Rose/reds in star: 2 1/8 yards
Green print (F and the binding): 1 1/2 yards
Rose plaid vine in border: 3/4 yard
Applique: A variety of rose/red scraps in varying sizes
Green stripe inner border: 1/3 yard
Backing and sleeve: 4 yards
Batting: 62" square
64 sheets of 8 1/2" x 11" vellum

Cutting Instructions

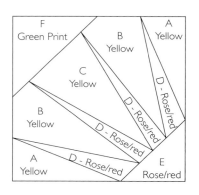

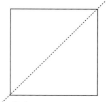

Subcut once, diagonally.

Yellow block and border backgrounds
A - Cut 16 strips 2 1/2" x 40", subcut 128 units 2 1/2" x 5"
B - Cut 22 strips 3" x 40", subcut 128 units 3" x 6"
C - Cut 11 strips 3 1/4" x 40", subcut 64 units 3 1/4" x 6"
Cut 4 border strips 6" x 52" (cut lengthwise)
Cut 4 border corner squares 6" x 6"

Rose/reds in stars
D - Cut 43 strips 1 1/2" x 40", subcut 256 units 1 1/2" x 6"
E - Cut 32 squares 3 1/8" x 3 1/8", subcut them in half once diagonally

Green print
F - Cut 32 squares 3 7/8" x 3 7/8", subcut them in half once diagonally
Cut a 30" square to make 2 1/2" wide continuous bias binding
   (See page 16 for instructions.)

Rose vine
Cut a 24" square to make 1 1/2" wide continuous bias stem
   (See pages 16-17 for instructions.)

Green stripe inner border
Cut 8 strips 1 1/4" x 40"

Foundation Paper Pattern

In foundation paper piecing you sew your fabric directly to a paper foundation. We like to sew to vellum. It is sturdy, yet easy to remove. It is translucent, making it easier to position fabric. Vellum works well in both copiers and computer printers.

You can find vellum at most hobby shops or at architectural supply shops. It comes in pads that are standard paper size. "Clear Print" is the brand we buy most often.

You have the option of tracing the foundation paper patterns by hand. This can be tedious and time consuming. It is faster and more accurate to copy the foundation paper patterns on a copier. If you use a copier, always check the first copy against the original to make sure you are getting an accurate copy.

Make 64 copies of this page on vellum. Carefully cut out each foundation paper on the outer dashed lines only. Each star is made up of 4 foundation paper pieced units.

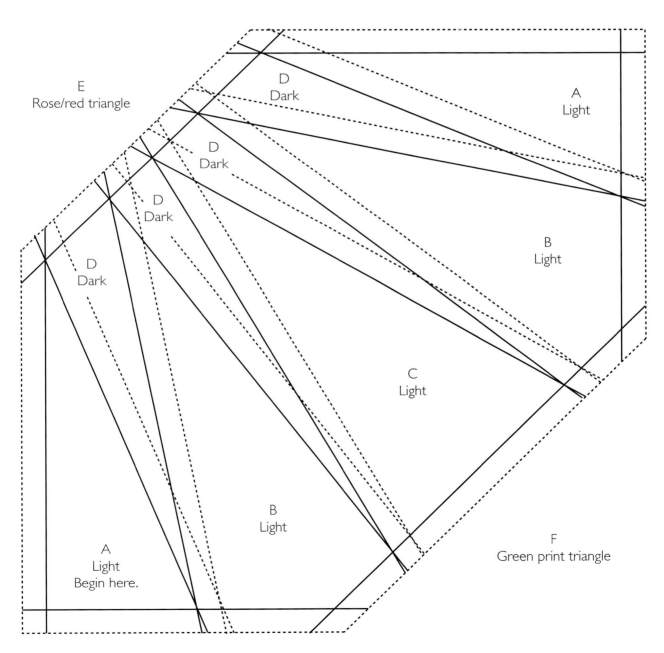

Foundation Paper Piecing

The dashed lines on the foundation paper pattern indicate where the raw edges of the fabric go. Solid lines indicate seam lines. Sew on the solid lines.

> *FYI...*
> *Sew with the drawn side of the paper facing up, toward you.*
> *The wrong side of the fabric is next to the wrong side of the paper.*
> *The fabric strips themselves are sewn right sides together.*

Set your sewing machine with a shorter-than-normal stitch length. Each time the needle pierces the paper, it perforates it. The more the paper is perforated, the easier the paper will be to remove. However, you don't want to have your stitch length so short that it is unattractive. Practice using different stitch lengths until you find the one that is best for your machine.

Try using a finer cotton thread than you normally piece with. Finer thread works better with the shorter stitch length. Test your thread and stitch length before starting on your real blocks.

Always make a test block! Once you are comfortable with the instructions, you can make the rest of the units in an assembly-line fashion.

Sew the Stars

Place a yellow A strip below the paper in position to cover the section marked "A, Light, Begin here" as shown below. The wrong side of the fabric is next to the paper.

Place a rose/red D strip under the yellow fabric strip as shown below. The fabric strips are always right sides together. Line up the edges of the fabric with the dashed line on the paper. The strips are offset so that when they are pressed open, the D strip will cover the D star point completely.

Sew on the solid line from one edge of the paper to the other.

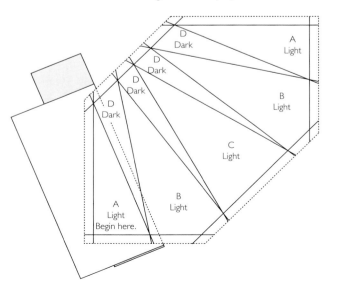

Press open. Trim away the excess D fabric. This is easier if you fold the foundation paper on the next dashed line and use the folded paper edge as a guide.

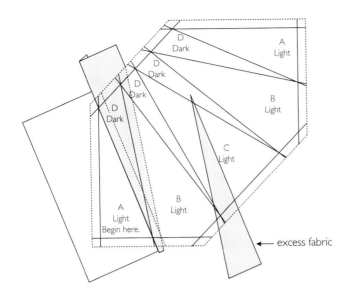

Position a yellow B strip as shown below. Remember that the fabric is always right sides together. Offset the B strip so that when it is pressed open all of it will cover the width of the B area completely.

Sew on the solid line from one edge of the paper to the other.

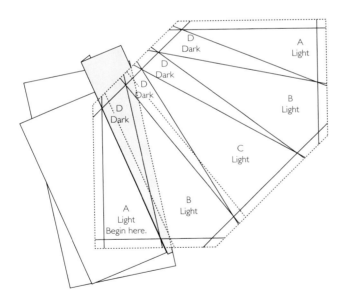

Press open. Trim away the excess B fabric as described above. Continue in this manner until all the foundation paper units have been pieced.

After the foundation paper units are complete, trim away the excess fabric from the edges of the paper. Using a ruler and rotary cutter will be faster, but be careful not to let your ruler move on the paper.

Center an E triangle over the base of the star points, right sides together. Pin in place to prevent movement. Sew with the paper side up. Trim away the little triangles that extend beyond the edges of the paper. Press open.

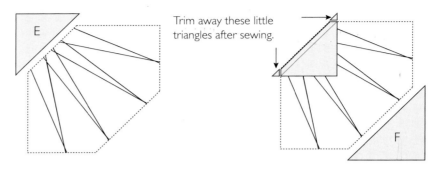

Sew an F triangle to the other side of each foundation paper unit as described above.

The pattern for the border is on the big pattern sheet at the back of the book. Applique the borders and the border corners. When your applique is complete, press your blocks and borders on the wrong side.

Set the center of the quilt together as shown below. Use positioning pins (see page 21) to match the star points perfectly. Sew the inner border strips together end-to-end, into pairs. The star blocks are heavily pieced. It is a good idea to measure the center of your quilt before cutting the inner and outer borders to size. Adjust the lengths of your inner and outer borders if necessary. Trim the borders as follows:

> Cut 2 side inner borders 1 1/4" × 48 1/2"
> Cut 2 the top and bottom inner borders 1 1/4" × 50"
> Trim the outer applique borders to 4 1/2" × 50"
> Trim the border corners to 4 1/2" square

Sew the borders to the quilt. Finish your quilt as described on pages 54-55.

The vine in the border is easy to make. Use the bias stem technique found on pages 16-17.

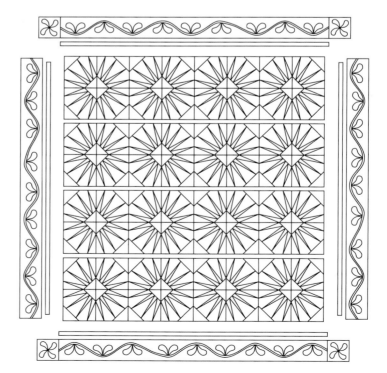

Waltzing Stars

Finished quilt size: 57 ¹/₂" square

Wowie Zowie! Yellow does perk up a quilt! Becky used three different yellow prints and many different rose/reds in the pieced stars. Notice the plaids and stripes inside the stars and the applique border. Quilters sometimes avoid fabric with lines because they worry that they will stand out too much. This quilt shows that linear fabric can accentuate the design without overpowering it.

Tossed Tulips

Finished quilt size: 58" square

Fresh tulips dance happily in a field of green. The prints and plaids are delightfully scrappy. The easy strip-pieced setting combined with the cute appliquéd tulips make this quilt a winner!

Pretty in Plaid

Finished quilt size: 57 ¹/₂" square

This quilt could also be called "Pretty in Pink!" The combinations of rose, red, wine, pink, and cream colors give this quilt a rosy glow. The variety of prints in the background provides a lively mix of visual textures. These textures contrast nicely with the plaids used in the applique. The greens and little bits of blue add just the right sparkle to the quilt.

Neapolitan Nights

Finished size: 44 $\frac{1}{4}$" square

*Chocolate, vanilla, and straw-
berry! Doesn't this quilt make you
think of Neapolitan ice cream! This
quilt is made entirely with plaids and
stripes.*

*Have some fun with the fabric in
the stars. We used plaids and stripes.
By fussy-cutting the diamonds, you can
create some wonderful designs. The
eight-point stars are pieced and then
appliqued to the block. It's just too easy!*

Lady of the Lake

Finished quilt size: 57" x 44 $\frac{1}{4}$"

*It's hard to believe that such a complex
looking quilt is really easy to make! Our
"contemporary" antique quilt is made from
vibrant blue plaids and stripes in combination
with a wheat-colored woven stripe. These
clean, clear colors bring the quilt to life!*

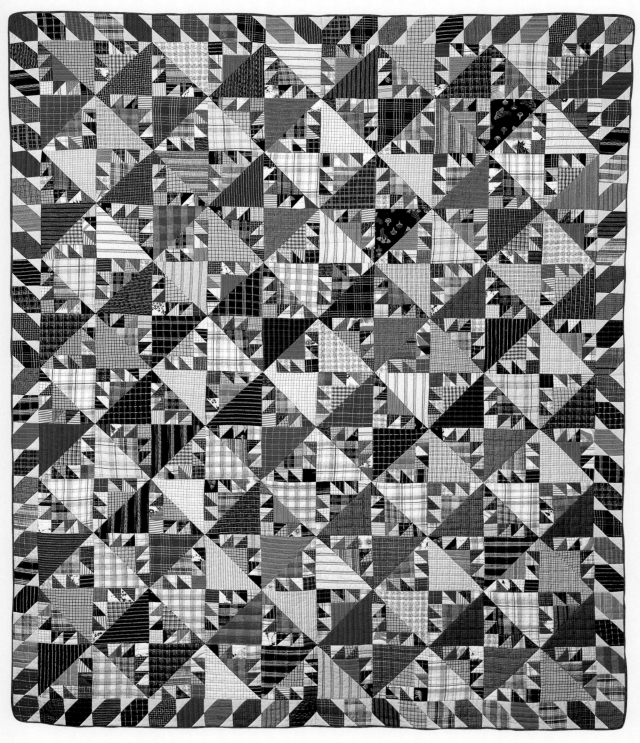

The Delectable Mountains

Finished quilt size: 66" x 78"

This scrap quilt is really a study in values. The arrangement of the light, medium, and dark fabrics in the blocks creates a wonderful secondary pattern. This quilt is comprised of many different plaids and stripes. Becky tossed in the occasional print just for fun! It is hand quilted in-the-ditch and on various lines in the plaids and stripes with burgundy quilting thread.

Royal Plumes

Finished quilt size: 36" square

We combined Nine-Patches and applique in this perky little quilt. Made entirely of woven plaids and stripes, this is a "planned" scrappy quilt. The colors in the Nine-Patches and in the borders are mostly random. However, the positioning of the dark rose triangle squares in the centers and corners of the borders combined with the blues in the plumes and the inner border create a subtle square-in-a-square design.

Meadow Green

Finished quilt size: 60" x 72"

Woven plaids and stripes (and one perky green dot) combine to create this easy happy, scrappy quilt. While this quilt is predominantly green, many other colors are woven into the plaids and stripes. You'll see orange, blue, purple, pink, gold - just like a meadow in bloom!

Simplicity

Finished quilt size: 56" square

This applique design, inspired by an antique quilt, is simple! The visual activity in the blue and cream prints in the background adds the spice. Linda created an interesting secondary design by alternating the position of the reds and blues in the applique blocks. Quilters who are nervous about using plaids and stripes should look closely at this quilt. The plaids are subtler than the prints!

SIMPLICITY

Finished applique block size: 16"
Finished border width: 4"
Finished quilt size: 56" square

This applique design, inspired by an antique quilt, is simple! The visual activity in the blue and cream prints in the background adds the spice. Linda created an interesting secondary design by alternating the position of the reds and blues in the applique blocks.

Materials
Block and border backgrounds: 3 5/8 yards
Red used in the applique: 2 1/4 yards
Blue used in the applique: 2 yards
Binding: 7/8 yard
Backing and sleeve: 4 yards
Batting: 62" square

Cutting Instructions
Block backgrounds
Cut 36 squares 9" x 9"
Border backgrounds
Cut 16 strips 6" x 8 1/2"
Cut 8 strips 6" x 10"
Cut 4 squares 6" x 6"
Applique piece #2 (Use the cutaway applique technique.)
Cut 5 red squares 13" x 13"
Cut 4 blue squares 13" x 13"
Blue vine
Cut a 24" square to make 1 1/2" wide continuous bias and bias stem
(See pages 16-17 for instructions.)
The remaining applique pieces are cut from the red and blue fabric.
Binding
Cut a 30" square to make 2 1/2" wide continuous bias binding
(See page 16 for instructions.)

Make the Quilt
The patterns for the blocks and border can be found on the large pattern sheet at the back of the book. Prepare your templates and overlays. Make your overlay for the whole 16" block as indicated on the pattern.

Play with the placement of the different block backgrounds on your design wall. The applique covers a lot of the background fabric, but it is still important that the backgrounds are visually balanced. When you are happy with the arrangement of the backgrounds, sew them together into 9 Four-Patches. Applique your blocks.

We used this versatile border in three very different quilts: *Simplicity*, *Pretty in Plaid*, and *Waltzing Stars*. This border is a little shorter than the others. The length is marked on the pattern. Sew 4 border backgrounds as shown below.

6" × 10"	6" × 8 1/2"	6" × 8 1/2"	6" × 8 1/2"	6" × 8 1/2"	6" × 10"

Applique the borders and the border corners. When your applique is complete, press your blocks and borders on the wrong side. Trim them as follows:

Trim applique blocks to 16 1/2" square

Trim the borders to 4 1/2" × 48 1/2"

Trim the border corners to 4 1/2" square

Set the parts of the quilt together as shown below. Finish your quilt as described on pages 54-55.

The vine in the border is easy to make. Use the bias stem technique found on pages 16-17.

PRETTY IN PLAID

Finished applique block size: 18"
Finished sashing width: 4 $\frac{1}{2}$"
Finished border width: 4"
Finished quilt size: 57 $\frac{1}{2}$" square

This quilt could also be called "Pretty in Pink!" The combinations of rose, red, wine, pink, and cream colors give this quilt a rosy glow (see page 35). The variety of prints in the background provides a lively mix of visual textures. These textures contrast nicely with the plaids used in the applique. The greens and little bits of blue add just the right sparkle to the quilt.

Materials

Block backgrounds: 1 $\frac{1}{8}$ yards or 16 different 10" squares
Light sashing and border backgrounds: 1 $\frac{5}{8}$ yards (cut all lengthwise)
Dark sashing: 1 $\frac{1}{2}$ yards (cut all lengthwise)
Brown vine in border: $\frac{3}{4}$ yard
Applique: A variety of fabric scraps in varying sizes
Plaid binding: $\frac{7}{8}$ yard
Backing and sleeve: 4 yards
Batting: 62" square
Dark pink embroidery floss used in Block #2

Cutting Instructions

Block backgrounds
Cut 16 squares 10" × 10"

Light sashing
A - Cut 2 strips 2" × 18 $\frac{1}{2}$"
B and C - Cut 3 strips 2" × 41"
D - Cut 2 strips 2" × 50"

Dark sashing
A - Cut 4 strips 2" × 18 $\frac{1}{2}$"
B and C - Cut 6 strips 2" × 41"
D - Cut 4 strips 2" × 50"

Border backgrounds
Cut 4 strips 6" × 52"
Cut 4 squares 6" × 6" (Cut last from remainder.)

Brown vine
Cut a 24" square to make 1 $\frac{1}{2}$" wide continuous bias and bias stem
(See pages 16-17 for instructions.)

Plaid binding
Cut a 30" square to make 2 $\frac{1}{2}$" wide continuous bias binding
(See page 16 for instructions.)

Make the Quilt

Play with the placement of the different block backgrounds on your design wall. When the backgrounds are visually balanced sew them together into 4 Four-Patches

The patterns for the blocks and border can be found on the large pattern sheet at the back of the book. Prepare your templates and overlay. "Audition" your applique pieces on the backgrounds on the design wall before you begin stitching. It's a lot easier to change fabrics before they are sewn down.

Applique your blocks, the borders, and the border corners. When your applique is complete, press your blocks and borders on the wrong side. Trim them as follows:

Trim applique blocks to 18 1/2" square

Trim the borders to 4 1/2" x 50"

Trim the border corners to 4 1/2" square

Sew the sashing units together from the strips you have cut. Be sure to use a 1/4" seam allowance. Set the parts of the quilt together as shown below. Finish your quilt as described on pages 54-55.

The vine in the border is easy to make. Use the bias stem technique found on pages 16-17.

NEAPOLITAN NIGHTS

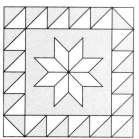

Finished block size: 9"
Finished triangle squares: 1 ¹/₂"
Finished border width: 3"
Finished quilt size: 44 ¹/₄" square

Chocolate, vanilla, and strawberry! Doesn't this quilt make you think of Neapolitan ice cream (see page 36)! The eight-point stars are pieced and then appliqued to the block. It's just too easy! Have some fun with the fabric in the stars. We used plaids and stripes. By fussy-cutting the diamonds you can create some wonderful designs in the stars.

Finished 9" block—
The sashing is part
of the block!

Materials

Chocolate brown plaid: 1 ¹/₄ yards
Strawberry red : 1 ¹/₂ yards
Vanilla: 1 ¹/₃ yard
Appliqued eight-point stars: Rose/red plaids and stripes in varying sizes
Plaid binding: ⁷/₈ yard
Backing and sleeve: 3 yards
Batting: 50" square

Cutting Instructions

Chocolate brown
Cut 12 squares 8" x 8" for the star block backgrounds
Cut 3 squares 9 ³/₄" x 9 ³/₄" for the triangle blocks
    Subcut in half diagonally twice to make 12 triangles
Cut 4 strips 1 ¹/₂" x 38 ³/₄" for the border
    Measure your quilt before cutting the borders to size!

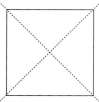

Subcut twice,
diagonally.

Strawberry red
Cut 19 strips 2" x 40"
    Subcut into 364 - 2" squares for the triangle squares
Cut 12 squares 2 ³/₈" x 2 ³/₈"
    Subcut in half diagonally once for the loose triangles
Cut 4 strips 1 ¹/₂" x 38 ³/₄" for the border
    Measure your quilt before cutting the borders to size!

Vanilla
Cut 19 strips 2" x 40"
    Subcut into 364 - 2" squares for the triangle squares
Cut 4 strips 1 ¹/₂" x 38 ³/₄" for the border
    Measure your quilt before cutting the borders to size!

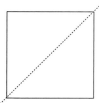

Subcut once,
diagonally.

Plaid binding
Cut a 30" square to make 2 ¹/₂" wide continuous bias binding
    (See page 16 for instructions.)

Sew the Stars

The pattern for the eight-point star can be found on the large pattern sheet at the back of the book. Prepare 2 diamond templates - 1 with a ¼" seam allowance and 1 without. Prepare an overlay for this block.

Lay the larger diamond template on the **wrong side** of your star fabric. Fussy-cut the diamonds. Look at the quilt on page 36 for inspiration. Trace 8 diamonds for every star. Cut these diamonds out on the drawn line. "Audition" the star pieces on the design wall before you begin stitching.

It is fast and easy to piece the eight-point stars on the sewing machine. When the stars have been pieced, applique them to the chocolate background blocks. When your applique is complete, press your blocks on the wrong side. Trim applique blocks to 6 ½" square.

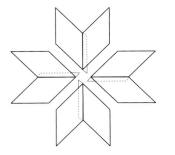

Sew the diamonds for 1 star together into pairs. Press all seam allowances in the same direction, so that they fan around the star.

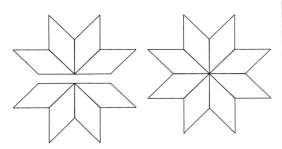

Sew pairs together to form the 2 halves of the star. Press. Sew the two halves of the star together. Press.

Turn the completed star right side up. Place the smaller template right side up on 1 diamond of the star. Trace around the 2 outer edges of the template. Repeat for each diamond in the star.

Use the overlay to position the star on the background block. Applique it in place as you would any other applique piece.

Make the Quilt

Make 364 triangle squares from the light and dark 2" squares (see page 18). Press the seam allowances to the dark side of the triangle square.

Gather all the parts of the quilt. Make the blocks as described on the next page. Pressing seams as indicated will lessen some of the bulk at the points when you sew the blocks together.

Pay close attention to the diagram when setting the quilt together. Make sure that the "top" of the block is pointing in the proper direction. Finish the quilt as directed on pages 54-55.

Press new seam allowances in the direction of the arrows.

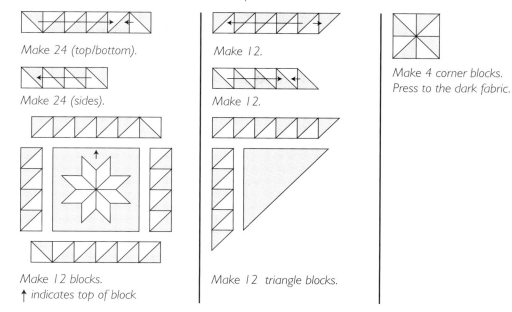

Make 24 (top/bottom).

Make 12.

Make 4 corner blocks.
Press to the dark fabric.

Make 24 (sides).

Make 12.

Make 12 blocks.
↑ indicates top of block

Make 12 triangle blocks.

FYI...

Put a pin at the "top" of each star block. Position the top of each star block as shown below. Take your time...

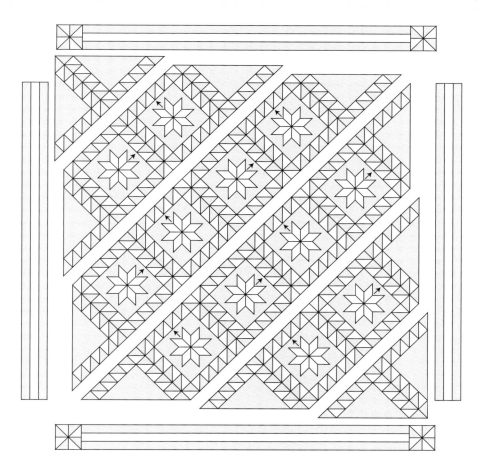

Sew dark-light-dark border strips together as shown at left. Measure your quilt top before cutting these borders to size.

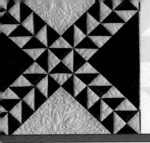

LADY OF THE LAKE,
VERSION 1.1

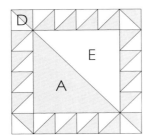

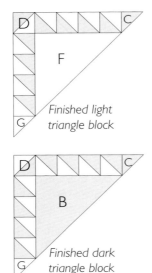

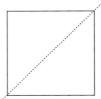

Finished block size: 9"
Finished triangle squares: 1 ¹/₂"
Finished border width: 3"
Finished quilt size: 57" x 44 ¹/₄"

It's hard to believe that such a complex *looking* quilt is really easy to make! Our "contemporary" antique quilt is made from vibrant blue plaids and stripes in combination with a wheat-colored woven stripe (see page 36). These clean, clear colors bring the quilt to life!

Materials

Blue plaids and stripes: 3 yards
Light woven stripe : 2 ⁵/₈ yards
Plaid binding: ⁷/₈ yard
Backing and sleeve: 4 yards
Batting: 61" x 50"

Cutting Instructions

Blue plaids and stripes

A - Cut 9 squares 6 ⁷/₈" x 6 ⁷/₈" for the large triangle squares
   Subcut in half diagonally once to make 18 triangles, discard 1
B - Cut 2 squares 9 ³/₄" x 9 ³/₄" for the triangle blocks
   Subcut in half diagonally twice to make 8 triangles
C - Cut 7 squares 2 ³/₈" x 2 ³/₈" for the small loose triangles
   Subcut in half diagonally once to make 14 triangles
D - Cut 25 strips 2" x 40"
   Subcut into 482 - 2" squares for the triangle squares
Cut 16 strips 1 ¹/₂" x 40" for the border, sew in pairs, center seam, cut to fit

Light woven stripe

E - Cut 9 squares 6 ⁷/₈" x 6 ⁷/₈" for the large triangle squares
   Subcut in half diagonally once to make 18 triangles, discard 1
F - Cut 2 squares 9 ³/₄" x 9 ³/₄" for the triangle blocks
   Subcut in half diagonally twice to make 8 triangles
G - Cut 7 squares 2 ³/₈" x 2 ³/₈" for the small loose triangles
   Subcut in half diagonally once to make 14 triangles
D - Cut 25 strips 2" x 40"
   Subcut into 482 - 2" squares for the triangle squares
Cut 8 strips 1 ¹/₂" x 40" for border, sew in pairs, center seam, cut to fit

Plaid binding

Cut a 30" square to make 2 ¹/₂" wide continuous bias binding
   (See page 16 for instructions.)

Finished 9" block

Finished light triangle block

Finished dark triangle block

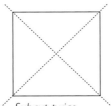

Subcut once, diagonally.

Subcut twice, diagonally.

Make the Quilt

Make 482 triangle squares from the light and dark 2" squares. Press the seam allowances to the dark half of the triangle square. Gather all the parts of the quilt. Make the blocks as described below. Pay close attention to the diagram when setting the quilt together. Finish the quilt as directed on pages 54-55.

 Make 17 from the 6 ⁷⁄₈" squares.

AND

Make 482 from the 2" squares.

Press new seam allowances in the direction of the arrows.

Make 34 (top/bottom).

Make 7.

Make 7.

Make 34 (sides).

Make 7.

Make 7.

Make 4 corner blocks. Press seams to the darker fabric.

Make 17 blocks.

Make 7 dark triangle blocks.

Make 7 light triangle blocks.

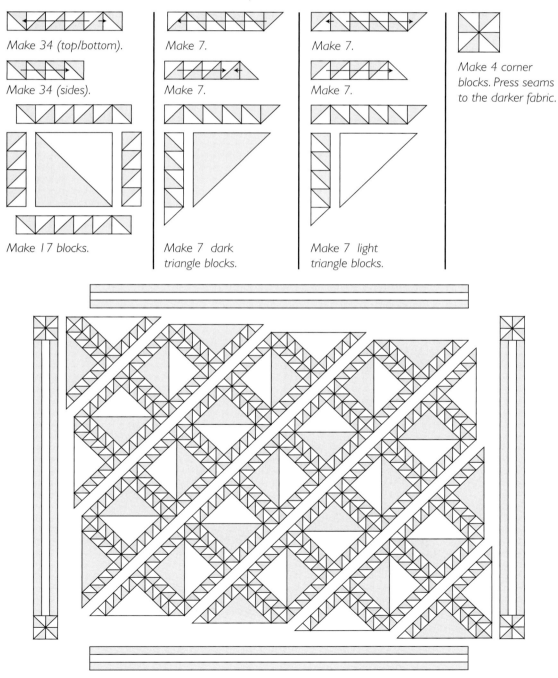

THE DELECTABLE MOUNTAINS

Finished block size: 6"
Finished border width: 3"
Finished quilt size: 66" x 78"

This scrap quilt is really a study in values (see page 37). The arrangement of the light, medium, and dark fabrics in the blocks creates a wonderful secondary pattern. This quilt is comprised of many different plaids and stripes. Becky tossed in the occasional print just for fun!

Materials
Light fabrics: 3 $^5/_8$ yards
Dark fabrics: 4 yards
Medium fabrics: $^3/_4$ yard
Plaid binding: $^7/_8$ yard
Backing and sleeve: 5 yards
Batting: 70" x 82"

Cutting Instructions

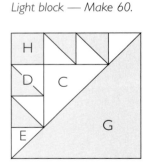

Light block — Make 60.

Light fabrics
  A - Cut 30 squares 6 $^7/_8$" x 6 $^7/_8$"
    Subcut in half diagonally once to make 60 triangles
  B - Cut 60 squares 2" x 2"
  D - Cut 24 strips 2" x 40"
    Subcut 480 squares 2" x 2"
  E - Cut 60 squares 2 $^3/_8$" x 2 $^3/_8$"
    Subcut in half diagonally once to make 120 triangles
  F - Cut 184 squares 2" x 2"

Dark fabrics
  G - Cut 30 squares 6 $^7/_8$" x 6 $^7/_8$"
    Subcut in half diagonally once to make 60 triangles
  H - Cut 60 squares 2" x 2"
  D - Cut 24 strips 2" x 40"
    Subcut 480 squares 2" x 2"
  I - Cut 60 squares 2 $^3/_8$" x 2 $^3/_8$"
    Subcut in half diagonally once to make 120 triangles
  J - Cut 92 squares 3 $^1/_2$" x 3 $^1/_2$"

Medium fabrics
  C - Cut 60 squares 3 $^7/_8$" x 3 $^7/_8$"
    Subcut in half diagonally once to make 120 triangles

Striped binding
  Cut a 30" square to make 2 $^1/_2$" wide continuous bias binding
    (See page 16 for instructions.)

Dark block — Make 60.

Border block — Make 92.

Make the Quilt

Make 480 triangle squares (D) from the light and dark 2" squares (see page 18). Press the seam allowances to the dark half of the triangle square. Gather all the parts of the quilt. Make the blocks as described below. Be careful not to stretch the bias edges of the triangles as you handle and sew them.

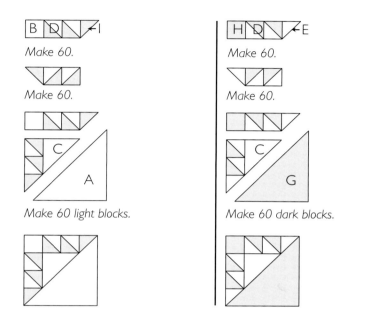

Make 60.

Make 60.

Make 60 light blocks.

Make 60.

Make 60.

Make 60 dark blocks.

Follow the instructions on page 19 to make the border blocks.

Make 92 border blocks.

Set 2 light blocks and 2 dark blocks together as shown in the upper left corner of the illustration below. Repeat for all blocks. Set the blocks together as shown below. Finish the quilt as directed on pages 54-55.

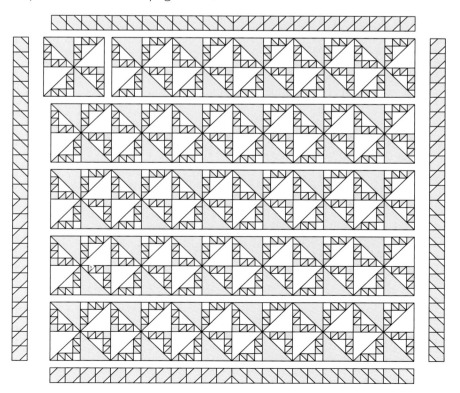

Finished Nine-Patches and Snowball block sizes: 6"
Finished inner border width: 1"
Finished outer border width: 2"
Finished quilt size: 60" x 72"

Woven plaids and stripes *(and one perky green dot)* combine to create this easy happy, scrappy quilt (see page 39). While this quilt is predominantly green, many other colors are woven into the plaids and stripes. You'll see orange, blue, purple, pink, gold - just like a meadow in bloom!

Materials

Light fabrics: 3 $1/4$ yards
Dark fabrics: 2 $3/4$ yards
Inner border fabric: $3/8$ yard
Plaid binding: $7/8$ yard
Backing and sleeve: 4 $3/4$ yards
Batting: 64" x 76"

Cutting Instructions

Light fabrics
> Cut 14 strips 2 $1/2$" x width of fabric (at least 40") for the Nine-Patches
>> Subcut strips in half (at least 20"), discard 1
> Cut 9 strips 6 $1/2$" x 40" for the snowballs
>> Subcut 49 squares 6 $1/2$" x 6 $1/2$"
> Cut 8 strips 2 $1/2$" x 40" for the outer border
>> Subcut 128 squares 2 $1/2$" x 2 $1/2$"

Dark fabrics
> Cut 17 strips 2 $1/2$" x width of fabric (at least 40") for the Nine-Patches
>> Subcut strips in half (at least 20"), discard 1
> Cut 13 strips 2 $1/2$" x 40" for the Snowballs
>> Subcut 196 squares 2 $1/2$" x 2 $1/2$"
> Cut 8 strips 2 $1/2$" x 40" for the outer border
>> Subcut 128 squares 2 $1/2$" x 2 $1/2$"

Inner border fabrics
> Cut 8 strips 1 $1/2$" x 40"

Binding
> Cut a 30" square to make 2 $1/2$" wide continuous bias binding
>> (See page 16 for instructions.)

Make the Quilt

Strip piece the Nine-Patches (see pages 20 and below). The more you mix up the combination of different fabric strips, the scrappier your quilt will look.

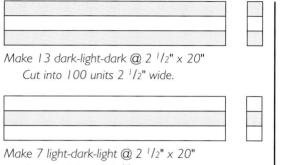

Make 13 dark-light-dark @ 2 1/2" x 20"
Cut into 100 units 2 1/2" wide.

Make 50 dark Nine-Patches.

Make 7 light-dark-light @ 2 1/2" x 20"
Cut into 50 units 2 1/2" wide.

Make the Snowball blocks (see page 19 and below). Press the seam allowances to the light center of the block.

Make the triangle squares for the border (see page 18). Press the seam allowances to the dark fabric.

Make 49 Snowball blocks from the light 6 1/2"
squares and from 196 dark 2°1/2" squares.

Make 128 triangle squares from the dark
and the light 2 1/2" squares.

Sew inner border strips end-to-end into pairs. Trim the inner borders as follows:

Cut 2 side inner borders 1 1/2" x 66 1/2".

Cut the top and bottom inner borders 1 1/2" x 56 1/2".

Assemble all of the parts of the quilt on your design wall. Play with the arrangement of the colors until you are happy with them.

Set the quilt together as shown at right. Finish your quilt as described on pages 54-55.

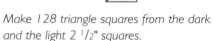

FINISH YOUR QUILT

Layer & Baste

Construct the quilt top as indicated in the directions. Make sure that the wrong side is clear of bits of fabric, thread, and other debris. Press the top (wrong side up) if it needs it.

Construct the back of the quilt. The back of the quilt should be about 2" bigger than the top on all sides. Lay the back right side down on a firm surface.

Lay your batting over the back. Pat out any wrinkles. Do not stretch the batting! Center the top right side up over the batting. Baste the layers together with a good quality thread. Cheap thread can leave stains on your quilt.

Quilt your quilt by hand or machine. We quilt with cotton thread when working on cotton fabric. Finish the outer edge with continuous bias binding. See below for binding tips and the next page for sleeve directions.

Mitered Corners

Make perfect mitered corners every time by following these easy directions:

At the corner, stop sewing 1/4" away from the edge of the quilt. Make 2-3 backstitches. Remove from machine.

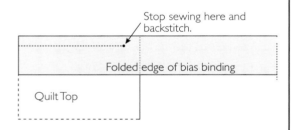

Stop sewing here and backstitch.

Folded edge of bias binding

Quilt Top

Fold the binding straight up at a 90° angle, creating a 45° fold in the binding.

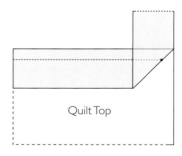

Quilt Top

Next, fold the binding straight down. Starting at the edge of the quilt top, continue sewing the binding to the quilt.

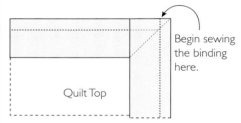

Begin sewing the binding here.

Quilt Top

Join the Ends

Cut the first end of the binding at a 45° angle. This end may be at a 45° angle already. Turn this end under 1/4" and press it.

Pin the beginning end of the binding to the middle of one side of the quilt. Begin sewing 4" from this end of the quilt. Sew the binding to the quilt.

When you get back to the beginning, overlap the ends of the binding and cut the other end off square. Be sure to leave the flat end long enough to be covered by the angled end of the binding.

Insert the end of the binding inside the angled first end of the binding. Pin in place and sew.

Finish the folded edge by hand as you are sewing the binding to the back of the quilt.

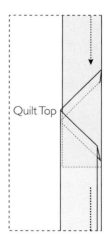

Quilt Top

Sleeve

Make and attach a sleeve to the back of the quilt. This will keep future generations from nailing your quilt to the wall! Once a sleeve is attached to a quilt, it is more likely to be hung properly. Following is the easiest way we know of to make and attach a sleeve.

Cut a strip of fabric 8 ½" wide and 2" less than the finished width of your quilt. *Measure your quilt to find its actual finished size.*

Turn under and hem both short ends of the sleeve. With wrong sides together, lay the sleeve on your ironing board and press it in half lengthwise.

Align the raw edges of the sleeve with the top raw edges of your quilt back. Pin it in place. The top edge of the sleeve will be sewn to the quilt back when you sew your binding to the quilt top. Finish the sleeve by blind stitching the sides and bottom of the sleeve to the quilt back.

Fold the sleeve in half, lengthwise. Press.
Center the sleeve on the top, back of the quilt. Pin it in place.

Sew these edges to the quilt.

← Hemmed end   Hemmed end →

Lengthwise fold

Back of quilt...

Documentation Patch

Make a documentation patch and sew it to the back of the quilt. Make sure you use permanent ink - or embroider the information! Include information that you want people to know about your quilt. Your name and address, the date, the fiber content of the quilt, if it was made for a special person or occasion - these are all things that can go on the documentation patch.

INDEX

Projects

Useful Information